HOW TO WIN AS A HIGH ROLLER WHILE LOSING YOUR SHIRT

By

Bernard Zeitler

2 MOON Press

Marshall - Michigan
800Publishing.com

How to Win as a High Roller while Losing Your Shirt

Cover design by Stephany Briceño

Layout by Kait Lamphere

Author photo courtesy of author

ISBN-13: 978-1-938110-83-2

First published in 2013

10 9 8 7 6 5 4 3 2 1

Published by 2 MOON PRESS
123 W. Michigan Ave, Marshall, Michigan 49068
www.800publishing.com

PRINTED IN THE UNITED STATES OF AMERICA

To all my fellow recovering addicts,
especially compulsive gamblers, and to
my Lansing GA friends and family,
thank you for your support.

CONTENTS

Introduction

What is your dream? What would you do if your dream came true? Compulsive gamblers go beyond all that. I know because I am a recovering compulsive gambler. My goal in writing this book goes beyond the story to the fantasy and how it looks over time, both in recovery and as the addict goes down the proverbial rabbit hole.

My name is Bernie, and I am a compulsive gambler. My chosen form of gambling - scratch off tickets. My last 'bet' was on November 21, 2007, yet I look back over my life and recognize early signs going back to about third grade.

To explain my recognition of childhood gambling signs, I first need to give the definition of Compulsive Gambling. Gambling is, as defined by GA (Gamblers Anonymous):

> Any betting or wagering, for self or others, whether for money or not, no matter how slight or insignificant, where the outcome is uncertain or depends upon chance or "skill."

That being said, during my childhood, I played marbles, go fish, and other games. I also took on other challenges such as eating, drinking (pop), and anything else for gain or personal recognition. These of themselves do not indicate compulsive gambling. However, when taken too seriously, they can indicate a problem in the making. The combination of the challenge and the thrill of competition helped promote the compulsion. When I was young, I played the games without any competitive focus until the challenge started to be a way to be accepted. When I was the winner, I received recognition. It became so enjoyable to be recognized for an accomplishment. It is difficult to believe that eating more food or drinking more soda pop than friends or class mates would give anyone a 'high,' but that is what began to happen.

Here is where I begin with the childhood high of being recognized for being better at something. In school, most of us just blend in. Even an athlete can find themselves blending into a bigger pool of all the area school athletes. One might stand out in a class of 25, but is that as far as it goes? Most people want to be appreciated at some level, but at what level does it stop? Sometimes even appreciation doesn't stop the desire to be the best. Compulsive gamblers and addicts go beyond that level to an escape from the life they are living. I will look at the process by following a poem I adapted from the poem: "Autobiography in Five Short Chapters" by Portia Nelson and with my original articles. After that, I will expand and talk about the newest lessons learned.

This is my adaptation for addiction and recovery....

Addiction and Recovery in Five Short Chapters

1.

I head toward my addiction.
The addiction is a deep hole
I fall into it.
I am lost... I feel helpless.
I blame others.
It takes forever to escape it.

2.

I head toward the addiction again.
The addiction is still a deep hole.
I pretend it does not exist.
I fall into it again.
I can't believe I am back in the hole,
but I still blame others.
It again takes forever to escape.

3.

I head toward the addiction again.
I see the deep hole of addiction.
I pretend it is not there.
I still fall in ...it is a patterned habit.
I see it clearly.
I know this place.
I take responsibility for it.
I escape immediately.

4.

I head toward the addiction again.
I see the deep hole of addiction
I avoid it at the last second.

5.

I change my path avoiding the addiction entirely.

Summarizing my 5 chapters

1.

I head toward my addiction.
The addiction is a deep hole
I fall into it.
I am lost... I feel helpless.
I blame others.
It takes forever to escape it.

This is the early process of the addiction. At this point, I am beyond the wish to stand out or be special. There comes a point where getting the high is all that matters and compulsive gamblers are no different. They chase the win with no regard for what happens at the end of the process. It does not matter how many other times they have been there... It only matters that the results are the same, yet they expect them to be different. There is no acknowledgment of having a problem, and when the gambling has run its course, it is a hole that causes the gambler to look for a way out and find scape goats to take the blame.

I lose because I do not have the best plan. No one is there to bring me luck, and yes, I cannot go home because no one cares. I couldn't find my way, and I feel hopeless. It is not my fault everyone else is not supportive or does not understand. Since I am not at fault, it is harder to find my way out, and often, I begin planning my return to 'win' my way out of this mess.

2.

I head toward the addiction again.
The addiction is still a deep hole.
I pretend it does not exist.
I fall into it again.
I can't believe I am back in the hole,
but I still blame others.
It again takes forever to escape.

There comes a time when addicts know that they are heading for trouble but don't want to believe it, so they keep going. Compulsive gamblers, like any addict, get to that point where chasing after the high is all that matters, even if they know that the letdown is coming. Here I am, gambling to escape the reality, and when I get to the letdown, I tell myself I did not see it coming. The reality is: I knew it was coming. I just ignored it, so when it happened, I could still blame others. At this point, addicts never really get out of the mess, but they do see an improvement to a plateau. At this point, others are beginning to see what is happening. However, the addict pretends that the problem does not exist, and those around the addict often don't know exactly what the problem is. It is my experience that this is a place where the addict is stuck for a long time.

3.

I head toward the addiction again.
I see the deep hole of addiction.
I pretend it is not there.
I still fall in ...it is a patterned habit.
I see it clearly.
I know this place.
I take responsibility for it.
I escape immediately.

This is the point at which the addict knows what is coming but does not look at it. I know what is coming. I know that it is a disaster, but I focus on the high. I ignore the past history until I get into the disaster. Once there, I take responsibility and get out of my mess. The problem, though, is that as long as I can see the next high, I'll go back. I have figured out my pattern and live as if it is all worth it. This can go on for years, and as with other addictions, the addict can revert to earlier chapters.

4.

I head toward the addiction again.
I see the deep hole of addiction
I avoid it at the last second.

This is the beginning of recovery. The addict knows s/he has a problem, and while s/he still heads down the path of destruction, s/he stops at the last second. It does not mean they don't use, but they stop as soon as they start. It does not get to the depth that it has in the past. Oddly this is the most dangerous stage of all because it is where 'slips' happen. Often, it is a point at which the addict is most disappointed with themselves. I had an experience with this after my first GA meeting which left me with a desire to never go back to that. Here is a great example of this chapter... I went to my first meeting, heard all the stories, passed the test but decided I was not that bad. So as a result I left the meeting and went directly to the convenience store to buy a scratch-off ticket. At the moment I purchased that ticket, I not only knew I had a problem but knew I did not want to go back down that path.

5.

I change my path, avoiding the addiction entirely.

This is the point where recovery is in place. The hardest part of recovery is not getting too confident in it. The paths addicts take changes, but even then, there are things to look out for. Even when they change the road they take, there can be potholes and road construction, so watching the new road requires the full attention of the addict just like driving on the road. It is likely that if the addict doesn't stay alert, they will either go back to the original addiction or pick up a new one. In the following pages, I hope to reveal my path in a way that shows what other addictions can move in to replace the old one.

Join my journey into the addiction world and what happens in recovery. Let's look at how you can win as a high roller while losing your shirt of denial. We will begin with the fantasy of the compulsive gambler.

The Fantasy World

The fantasy of the compulsive gambler in the beginning is that they will be able to win big and help make life easier for others and themselves. The dream is truly a fantasy that rarely becomes a reality. For me, there was no reality for the fantasy, and it went to the place no one looks at in life.

When someone starts to plan for the future, no one says "oh I'll bury myself in debt" or "It would be fun to be broke." I started gambling in high fashion when I started seeing a day when I would no longer have to worry about what my job was. I began to believe that I'll win enough big bets to take care of everything. Over time, the fantasy became a false reality for me.

When I was in high school, the state was just starting their lottery programs, and I would buy one every so often but really focused on other stuff. My addiction at that time was just for fun and continued for almost two decades as such. During that time, I tried smoking, alcohol, and dealt with an eating problem. I still struggle with over-eating, but I never let the other stuff get a hold of me enough. As time went on, I found myself enjoying the time scratching off the tickets. I never really had the patience for the lottery drawings.

It started at some point with a "few minutes" of scratch-off tickets before I went home. How realistic is it to believe that I was going to hit the big win? Looking back on it, I wish that lightning would have struck before November of 2007, but it did not happen that way. The fantasy of winning big is less likely than being hit by lightning, but most, if not all, gamblers begin with the fantasy of beating the odds.

Once I started actively chasing the dream of a big win, I was off to the races. Looking back, I wish I had never entered the race. In November 2007, I had won that race. I started to recover from the biggest most self-destructive problem in my life. Today, I still fight for a recovery that is one day at a time and sometimes one minute at a time.

The "chase" is a fantasy world that deals with a selfish side of life. I felt guilt because of my own failures, and ultimately, this low self-image drew me deeper into the "chase." Gambling was my escape from arguments and the feelings of inadequacy. I could play scratch-offs and enter a dream world of being someone special. I could escape into the wood work for a short period. Twenty, thirty or forty dollars or more later, I'd head home knowing that my ex-wife would be asleep, and I felt I would get peace. To this day, I fail to understand how my gambling comforted me, yet I know it did until the very last bet.

My fantasy world came crashing down in late 2007, and now I am trying to build my life on realities as best I can. I looked to gambling to provide solutions for problems ranging from self-esteem to companionship. My ex-wife had told me that I had an affair with gambling and I cannot deny that. I deluded myself by dreaming of giving my family security financially through gambling in the beginning, yet at some point, the "chase" became my best friend, my lover, and a part of who I was.

The fantasy is over for me that I'll provide for my family all they need through my lover – the scratch-off ticket.

Thoughts and Reflections

My walk of Recovery and The Pain that Surfaced

I am a compulsive gambler and have an addictive personality, which means that I must work on having a higher awareness of what I am doing and know my weaknesses. As a person with an addictive personality, I can easily fall back into an addiction even if it is not the one I am recovering from. People have said that addiction is hereditary, and this is only half true. It is not addiction that is hereditary, but the tendency to be addicted. Below is my story after which I will discuss where I am in recovery today.

I have heard it said by others: "Addiction is Addiction is Addiction." No matter what the addiction, it is all the same. For that reason all addicts have to be aware of the triggers that could start them on the path to a new addiction.

I have to agree with the idea that once someone has been addicted to anything, they have to watch out for cross-addiction. For example, when a smoker quits smoking, they often begin to over eat. If an addictive personality begins the recovery process, they must become aware of the possible substitutions that may come into play.

While addiction has a genetic component, it can and usually is triggered by an initial choice to try that which is the addiction of choice. Before an addiction can happen, there has to be an exposure situation which means that the person has to have an experience. Oddly enough, it does not have to be a good experience to result in the addictive behavior.

I can look back over the years and see that I've been addicted to a number of things. The recovery I am going through today is from gambling. Much of addiction starts off as a past time. It's all in fun. Most addicts, myself included, say it all started with a recreational action. For instance:

- I'm only a social drinker.
- I only spend a little on gambling.

- I just tried one joint.
- I am only doing this because of peer pressure.
- I only smoke once in a while.

The problem is that once an addiction starts, the addict builds up a tolerance, and it takes more to achieve the same feeling. People start to relax and get away from problems for a while. Ultimately, the excuses start. Two such excuses are:

- I don't have a problem.

I am a responsible...

- This covers up the problem because as I said, the tolerance levels go up.

My addiction to gambling started as just one ticket and grew into a problem over time. Early on I was a 'binge' gambler, but as time went on, the 'binges' became more frequent and more expensive. By the end, it was no longer just 'binging' it was an almost continuous desire for the gambling.

Gambling: The Pit at The End of The Road

In late 2007, I came home from work a lost soul. My gambling had been out of control for many months, and now I had been sent home from work to await my fate. I was looking at being fired because of cash drawer shortages. My manager at the time knew I did not steal and was a good worker. He told me who to contact in order to fight for my job back. Over the next two days, I did fight for my job and was kept with the company. However, it meant that I would be moved to a different store.

A few days after losing my job, I was reinstated and scheduled to return to work at a new store. After a few years more working there, I left the job. I ended up spiraling down into a deep depression and before returning to work in 2007, I was admitted to the Adult Psych

Ward for Suicidal Depression. This would be my home for ten days, and I spent the time working on returning to "normalcy."

By the time I was admitted, I had "come clean" with my ex-wife about gambling. I was mortified because during our short courtship and the early years of our marriage (from 1987 to1995), I watched my mother-in-law spend excessive amounts of money on scratch-off lottery tickets and swore I would never do that. The problem was that now I had become the very thing I swore I would not. My ex-wife saw the pit of my depression that I had struggled with for years on this day. She did not see the level of depression that was often there, but in November of 2007, it was all out in the open, and during the ten days I was out of the house, she grew to see the home as calmer. She discovered by cleaning out my car, looking at finances, and doing the math just how bad things were because of my addiction.

I on the other hand was still in denial of the problem being *all* mine in this area. Gambling can start as a past-time and not be a real problem, but it can and often does change suddenly. I remember gambling a little since being in high school. Through to 1995, it was clearly not a problem because I may have spent all of $5.00 to $10.00 a year on this stuff with the rare increase to as much as $30.00 a year. The problem was that at some point, I became blind to my gambling and did it to escape my problems in the marriage.

On November 16, 2007 (my mother's birthday), I was discharged from the adult Psych Ward and returned home a smaller person with less depression and on medications for Bipolar disorder because the cloud of depression had been lifted. I look back on that ten days as a turning point for me while I still have a long way to go, this time, I'd changed my path.

On November 21, 2007, I attended my first GA meeting and proceeded to spend $1.00 on a scratch off ticket after the meeting. This also was a turning point for me. My thoughts when I left that first meeting were that I do not really have a problem. When I purchased that $1.00 ticket, I crumbled because I saw the lie of "I don't have a problem." Since that day, I have not had the urges like I had been, and whenever I start thinking I have licked the problem, I remind myself of that first GA meeting and of the ten days in Adult Psych.

Bottom line if a person denies having a problem but has the symptoms, they are only hurting themselves in this denial. The gambling, however, hurts family, friends, and work. Beyond this, it hurts all of society ultimately because of the things that tend to happen as a result.

If someone you know or you gamble, ask these Twenty Questions in regards to them or yourself:

(These are the questions asked of all new members of Gamblers Anonymous)

- Did you ever lose time from work or school due to gambling?
- Has gambling ever made your home life unhappy?
- Did gambling affect your reputation?
- Have you ever felt remorse after gambling?
- Did you ever gamble to get money with which to pay debts or otherwise solve financial difficulties?
- Did gambling cause a decrease in your ambition or efficiency?
- After losing, did you ever feel you must return as soon as possible and win back your losses?
- After a win, did you ever have a strong urge to return and win more?
- Did you often gamble until your last dollar was gone?
- Did you ever borrow to finance your gambling?
- Have you ever sold *anything* to finance gambling?
- Were you ever reluctant to use "gambling money" for normal expenditures?
- Did gambling make you careless of the welfare of yourself or your family?
- Did you ever gamble longer than you had planned?
- Have you ever gambled to escape worry or trouble?
- Have you ever committed or considered an illegal act to finance gambling?
- Did gambling cause you to have difficulty sleeping?

- Do arguments, disappointments, or frustrations create within you an urge to gamble?
- Did you ever have an urge to celebrate any good fortune by a few hours of gambling?
- Have you ever considered self-destruction or suicide as a result of your gambling?

Further have you ever thought any of the following?

- "The next one is a winner."
- "I know I'm getting close."
- "I can stop whenever I want."
- "I need to win today because I need the money."

I answered the twenty questions with some clarity but later realized and now remind myself daily that the truth is that all twenty questions are true when I am honest with myself. When I answered them the first time publicly, I answered **False** to about five. If you are a gambler or know someone who is, be honest with yourself because while gambling that is the biggest challenge. Gambling starts out as a choice but becomes a hunger until the problems pile up and the truth hits.

The Twenty Questions are asked of every new member of Gamblers Anonymous. It is said that most gamblers will answer yes to at least seven of them (that is less than 50%). My experience is that in the long run, many of us could see our life through a yes to all Twenty Questions.

The statements are things I've told myself to justify my actions. What is really sad is that I lied to myself and believed the lies.

Many gamblers are liars who lie to themselves so well that they begin to believe the lies. It is necessary to cover oneself when gambling mostly because deep down, they know that what you are doing is wrong.

My biggest challenge since starting on the road to recovery has been being honest with myself and those closest to me. The biggest loss is my ex-wife's trust. I may never get it back, and even today, there are struggles to battle the anger I have at myself. The anger was projected often on to my ex-wife because I no longer had any control of finances. I battle to regain my own self-respect and individualism while I was feeling trapped and hopeless about my marriage relationship.

Recovery for a gambler is like trying to cut off a diseased appendage in the Old West.

Thoughts and Reflections

Thoughts and Reflections

Addiction: The Sum Total of Recovery

My addiction to gambling started as just one ticket and grew into a problem over time. Early on I was a 'binge' gambler but as time went on the 'binges' became more frequent and more expensive. By the end it was no longer just 'binging' it was an almost continuous desire for the gambling. I note a number of points that are now going to be revisited. I noted the government's part in the addiction to gambling. This applies to any legal addiction. The list below is of legal and accepted addictions.

- Alcohol
- Smoking
- Gambling

This is not a complete list, but these three alone bring in more tax revenue for government entities equal to or greater than any taxes on income.

In Michigan, alcohol sales are connected to liquor licenses, sales taxes, and hidden taxes related to sales buried in the price of the alcohol, and let's not forget DUI and other tickets that can be issued as a result of the consumption of alcohol. Likewise many Alcoholics smoke as well as the two addictions go together. Remember how you used to go to a bar and people would also be smoking.

Cigarettes are sold at prices that are close to 60% taxes and then on top of that, there is a state sales tax. Since Gambling has become legal it has proliferated in the bars so it would seem that all three were together for al long time. As smoking was cut back in public places Gambling seems to be growing in the form of Club Keno, Card Games and people who are watching games they have wagers on.

The lottery is a significant income maker because the majority of the money brought in is profit. Retailers are not making much on this revenue item unless the winning tickets are sold there.

Casinos are another avenue for profit as the Government has to approve those not operated by Indian Tribes and even those run by the Indians have payouts for the government. These are things I see in recovery which have supported the idea that some addictions are acceptable to government agencies because they make money on the addict's misfortune. The more I use or do the behavior the more the money comes in to government coffers.

It is sad that often addicted individuals don't realize the problem until they are at the lowest possible point. I vowed not to be like my mother-in-law and yet today I am recovering from the very addiction she had. All addiction ultimately leads to the same places—Prison, Insanity, or Death.

My path to recovery travels through insanity.. Gambling made my depression worse ultimately. It drove me to a place of insanity. I created my own prison that I am still working to be released from today. Not all prisons are buildings. For example, I am in the prison of failure because of gambling.

What I mean by a prison of failure is that personal character flaws and past mistakes have been a stumbling block in my marriage, my relationships with family members, and my job situations. The gambling that I did overshadows my daily life. My ex-wife no longer trusts me, and my sons, who already did not like me, have a greater aversion to me, and I almost lost my job over gambling.

The cost of gambling is so great that it brings down even the best of people. The jobs it creates are more than just the obvious ones at the casinos and lottery commissions. Because of the problems associated with gambling, jobs are created in jails, prisons, hospitals, and private counseling offices around the country and world.

Addiction has a generic component to it that is genetic The genetic predisposition to addiction all starts with a choice, which ultimately destroys lives. Another friend talks as follows: I am a compulsive gambler choosing not to gamble. Further, the true addict in recovery knows that they can't just stop at one if they try it again. It is clear that while addiction is genetic, it is only the predisposition, and the addict makes an initial choice to try it.

An Open Letter from a Compulsive Gambler

Dear Readers,

I am writing to you in letter format to both apologize for my gambling and to give help to those who know a compulsive gambler that needs help.

As a compulsive gambler, I am acknowledging that my gambling may have influenced another person to start gambling. As a result of my gambling, I may have inflicted suffering on others who started because of my example and their family and friends to suffer just as those around me suffered. I know that there are those who were affected beyond my circle of influence, and while I cannot force someone to gamble, my actions could have encouraged it.

I also apologize to my ex-wife, sons, and family and friends who have had to put up with my absence and mood swings. My ex-wife and sons also have dealt with the worst possible consequences because of my gambling. My ex-wife lost financial security, and my sons lost opportunities to do things that they would have wanted to do. All the pain I caused my family can never be changed. It is my desire to change today and the future to cause no more harm. I hope that I can provide hope to those who are now dealing with addictive behavior.

I offer this advice to the gambler:

- Seek help before it gets too bad.
- Acknowledge that $1 lost is more than you can afford because once you start, it is hard to stop.
- Let family and friends know you need their help.

To the person dealing with a gambler:

- Look for ways to reach out to the gambler.
- Don't loan or help them financially.
- Be supportive of them if they are seeking help.

- If they don't acknowledge the problem, get other family and friends to help you with an intervention.
- If your state offers free or low cost counseling, seek it out for you and encourage the gambler to do likewise.

Finally, I give this hope: Help is available.

Check out these resources:

- Gamblers Anonymous
- Michigan Compulsive Gambling
- Never Enough

I sincerely hope to be of help to anyone who needs it.

Recovering With the help of God,

Bernard Zeitler

Thoughts and Reflections

Thoughts and Reflections

A New Beginning: 2012

So far, I have shared my prior writings on my addiction and the process of recovery, including what I felt was necessary as a part of my amends. As we go forward, I will talk more generally about compulsive gamblers in respect to the overall experiences and work on building a template of what could be a new future for recovery.

Compulsive gamblers have gone to the point of creating a new world where they continually chase the high of winning. The problem is that one win is not enough so they keep chasing it until they are broke and then they work on it with whatever means they can find. It is not always a financial "broke" that promotes the whatever-it-takes mode as there are other losses that are destructive. I discussed them in the open letter above. It becomes difficult to keep friends and relationships when the gambling takes the path of addiction.

Ask yourself: what would you do to escape problems? Oddly, that could become your personal addiction. With the compulsive gambler that is to some extent the case. Today I am in recovery and working on starting to rebuild what was lost. My losses were superficially financial but realistically far more severe. I lost my self-respect, the people closest to me, and time that would have been with others. Toward the end, I missed time with my mother who died on January 17, 2007, just ten months before I went into recovery. What I would not do to change that and live some of it over to spend time with her. This is my new beginning!

Today, I have been working very hard at rebuilding relationships with my two sons and reevaluating what the future looks like. My desire is to see compulsive gambling treated as any other addiction would be and trying to catch the signs before the losses of life, relationships and money (purposely in that order) become too great to turn around.

Today there are things that are private matters, but I keep very few secrets. I cannot afford to go back to where I was, so I have to plan a different path. The problem with that is that I have to keep my eyes open to other potential problems. Part of that is looking at fallacies that are a part of addiction and also a part of human nature.

Topics include the following:

- Id, Ego and, Super-Ego
- Gamblers Can Just Stop
- Sporadic Gambling Is Not Addicted Gambling

Other topics:

- Gambling Lies and Secrets
- Recovery
- Amends
- A Lifetime of Work
- Relapse
- Inevitable on Your Own
- The Need for Support
- Cross Addiction
- Co-Addictive Relationships

Thoughts and Reflections

Thoughts and Reflections

Id, Ego, and Super-Ego

First let's make a chart:

Id = I want— no thought about right or wrong. Based on the Pleasure Principle.

Ego = How can I please the id while being realistic about it and avoiding the consequences? How can I balance what I (id) want with reality?

Super-ego = Very clearly opposes the id and actively infers right and wrong. Will oppose the ego when it leans too closely to the id.

Ultimately, the principle is that the ego is the mediator between the other two. The problem for addicts is that the 'I want' tends to win. Recovery is a lifelong journey to regain a balance. As such, it is necessary to look at the id and super-ego as the extremes. Neither of these can have an abundant control.

If for instance an addict feels down, the id might say, 'Let's just do it!' The super-ego says, 'No, that is not good. Remember how much pain you had the last time?' The ego listens to both sides and says. 'How about this?' Translation... I want to gamble because life sucks right now... No way, you shouldn't do that. It is wrong, and the last time ... happened! Well how about I go to a movie with friends?

Result— going to the movies with friends, which could be far better. Let's say that instead the id wins, and I go gamble. I start out feeling good, but by the end, it ends up the same as in the past, and I feel horrible now. For that matter, I feel worse in the end than when I started. Now what happens if the super-ego wins? I don't go gambling, and I don't do anything else either. I was down before, and I remain down. I might just sit there mulling over everything, and let's say the conclusion is I am an awful person. What happens now?

I have heard it said that you want more id when in recovery and you are feeling down. I want the think-it-through process going on because there are other problems out there. Let's say it is not about gambling or a present addiction but rather about spending money on myself. Could the same problem end up being a part of the result? I.e. Could I become a spender and lose control of that? The answer is yes. I have the potential to become addicted to something else while in recovery from gambling, and undoubtedly, if I do not take the initiative to be aware of it I will find the substitute.

There is plenty of evidence for 'cross addiction.' If you have been in a Casino or other venue where gambling is going on, what else do you see? How about this: Food, alcohol, and at one time, smoking. So, compulsive gamblers could also be over-eaters, alcoholics, or smokers. Oddly, compulsive gamblers may also be recovering from these addictions as well. I have heard people in recovery from other addictions discount gambling as a possible problem. However, almost no compulsive gambler will discount the crossing over to another addiction. The topic of 'cross addiction' will be discussed in detail later. However the id, ego, and super-ego thought process needs to be realized before getting there.

Since addiction is often an issue of controlling a desire for a high, there is a natural draw to find a substitute high that was and is my curse in recovery. I need to be aware of that desire for a high to avoid it with a new addiction. Are there things that are desirable and make you feel good that could distract you from other interactions? Even now, I urge people to become aware of these hidden draws.

Thoughts and Reflections

Thoughts and Reflections

Gamblers Can Just Stop!

Most recovering compulsive gamblers have heard that phrase. People think that we can just stop but do not think the same of over eaters, alcoholics, or most other addictions. Let's say you love reading books, and you find one that is very compelling. People say that it is so good they just 'can't put it down.' Can you think of something that is so compelling or enjoyable that you get lost in it, and time gets away from you? The compulsive gambler is in that place. Often, they can't stop until the money runs out (until the end). In recovery, the compulsive gambler is fighting a desire that for them is as necessary as breathing. If it is looked at like that, can you just stop breathing? The only difference between breathing and addiction is that breathing is necessary and the addiction is believed to be necessary for the addict. In the case of compulsive gambling, even when the person becomes aware, it can still be hard to quit. I went to my first meeting and heard stories of what losses others had experienced and proceeded to buy a lottery ticket when I left the meeting. I consider that moment a life saver because I immediately broke down and realized I could not continue on the path I was on.

A compulsive gambler seldom talks about the losses and almost always talks about the wins. It is part of the illusion that has to be supported to keep doing what they are doing. The worst part is that as I stated earlier with my open letter, it brings others into the fantasy and expands the wake of destruction. Have you ever watched someone gambling and seen them win? How about losing? Do the promoters of gambling ever have a commercial showing someone losing to promote the business? Would that make you go there? The answers are obvious. At least they should be to anyone who desires to be free of addiction or knows someone with an addiction.

How about this for a comparison? Weight Loss programs tell about the people who are successful but not so much about the failures. If the success story ends up gaining the weight back, who do you hear it from? People do not like to admit failure or relapse. The programs are not eager to tell about them because that would discredit them.

If you lost weight on a program, you have a success story everyone wants to hear, but when you gain it back, do they want to hear it? Does the weight gain get reported, and if it does, is it accredited to the program or to the failure of the individual?

There is sporadic success and failure. Does this change the fact that the person is overweight?

Thoughts and Reflections

Thoughts and Reflections

Sporadic Gambling Is Not Addicted Gambling

While working on recovery, I have heard a term used that is to me very silly: Harm Reduction. It means being able to gamble with limits. It is a belief that someone can learn to control the urge to gamble to the point of reasonable limits. Consider this: is this possible with alcoholics, drug addicts, or smokers to stop at a safe point?

I agree with someone I met in recovery who said, "why stop at one?' You can't get the high with one lottery ticket, one drink, one cigarette, or one pill so what is the point? If someone goes out to eat can they fill up with one fry, onion ring, or other appetizer? No, they go there to get a meal not a single item. They don't go there, order a single piece of appetizer, and then leave. Why would anyone stop before they get the 'buzz' or 'high' that they have become accustomed to? Why would someone take one bite of a burger? They won't be full, which is why they bought the burger.

I started off with a scratch-off ticket every now and then. It did not go to the extreme from the beginning. Just like with other addictions, it started out slow, and as time went on, it took more to get the same feeling. At the end, it did not matter how much I gambled. I could not get to the same point. My point is that it started out just for fun and random and ended up over the top.

So much of compulsive gambling is hidden until it is too late because it is not usually recognized as a problem. It is clearly acceptable and is growing in popularity on so many levels. The governmental agencies enjoy huge tax gains, so they are not likely to stop. There is a part of the government conscience that makes sure there is help out there for those who want help, but generally speaking, it is not strong enough to say no way. In the United States, there are only two states that do not have legalized gambling (Hawaii and Utah). In the 1970's, only two states had legalized gambling, and oddly, it all started in Nevada because of the Great Depression. As financial recovery for Nevada was spurred by it over the last thirty years of the 20th century, other states began to take notes from Nevada and then New Jersey.

The point to this is that compulsive gamblers could not be gambling regularly in the early years because it took more travel or was limited by accessibility. As time has passed, accessibility has increased and thus the frequency and acceptability has also become more the norm. Just as alcoholism has always been there (even during prohibition), so compulsive gambling has always been there. The more acceptable it became, the more visible it became. Amazingly, as gambling began to show signs of helping economic growth, the state governments saw it as an income stream. The problem to consider is at what cost? Financial destruction of compulsive gamblers, crime rates, and tax evasion? The destructive forces will be discussed in my next section. For now, I want to talk about sporadic or occasional gamblers. These are the once a month or 'special event' gamblers, and I would propose that many have a problem as well.

Today there are multiple ways to gamble, and there are people who have a favorite form, but I also know that gambling is gambling no matter what form it takes. If a person gambles at the casino once in a while, they are at risk. That risk goes up if between these times, they 'occasionally' gamble in one or more other ways. The other ways include sports betting, state lotteries, bingo, family or friends poker nights, or any other form imaginable. The problem is that I can't say what the other forms might be because there are forms of gambling that are a matter of individual design. What I am referring to are ways that mimic what I talked about from my youth: Competitions that may not have any money involved such as drinking, eating, or any other form of compulsive competitions. So let's say an individual goes to the casino because it's fun occasionally, and between those visits, they buy scratch-off tickets occasionally. Then let's say between those scratch-offs, they play bingo and/ or private poker games. There is a high probability that the person has a problem, but the call has to be by the individual as no one can convince gamblers they have a problem until they get to a bottom that is personal. The hardest thing to do is to find a compulsive gambler if they don't want to be found. Other forms of addiction are seen because of the effects of the ingested substance. However, a compulsive gambler has signs that do not raise the same red flags. They are seen in the lies and secrets in the gamblers life, both their own and those of the people around them.

Thoughts and Reflections

Thoughts and Reflections

GAMBLING LIES AND SECRETS

The world is full of lies and secrets: a sad truth but more so for compulsive gamblers and those around them. The compulsive gambler has a web of lies that support the fantasies and hide the problem. They have secrets that allow them to hide what is behind the fantasy. Just as bad is that the people in the gambler's life often build their own lies and secrets to protect themselves from the gambler in their life and/or their own problem gambling.

The first clear lie for a compulsive gambler is "I do not have a problem, and I can quit at any time." At the time of my writing this book, this is still the view of most judges, probation officers, and a majority of the people who encounter the compulsive gambler. While there are many people who can stop at will, there are others who, like alcoholics, cannot stop so easily. The problem is that many compulsive gamblers have other coexisting addictions or have recovered from one addiction only to find gambling as a substitute.

Many people I have met have had other addictions and or mental health issues before the gambling. I can honestly say that I am no exception to that. Over the years, I tried smoking, drinking, and a few other similar addictions, which never really worked for me. There were some that worked well though, including but not limited to eating, Mountain Dew, and chocolate. I also have the diagnoses of ADHD and Bi-Polar with the main focus on long-term depression. This being said the mental health diagnoses are not the main focus in this, and I will address many of the lies and secrets from a purely addiction perspective.

Here are some other lies of the compulsive gambler:

1. I am doing this to make life better for others.
2. I have a system.
3. I am a winner.
4. I'll win my losses back.
5. I don't need to stop.
6. I can gamble just a little.

7. What I am doing is not gambling.
8. I'm not like the losers.
9. I can pay back what I owe.
10. My family will understand why I am not able to be there for...

As I said, there are lies related to those around the compulsive gambler too. Some of those are:

1. He/She works hard. They deserve an outlet.
2. He/She is not that bad.
3. We have fun when we are there together.
4. I like all the comps.
5. There is nothing wrong with having a little fun.

Both the compulsive gambler and those around them have a vested interest in living with these lies. Part of it is that they believe them, and part is that to accept the truth makes the whole world crash down around them. As I had said earlier, no one goes into their adult life and says, "Oh I'll bury myself in debt" or "It would be fun to be broke." These lies are without a doubt the path to that kind of statement. In my experience, some gamblers have people close to them who are unwittingly enablers by living their own secret lies.

As a compulsive gambler, I can say that when it all starts, there is a misconception that you will win and do wonderful things with those winnings. My vision was that my family would have everything they needed, that I would be able to help my church and give to causes for a long time to come. I also dreamed of traveling without worry where ever I wanted and whenever I wanted.

I remember my system when I started, and in the end, all I wanted to do was gamble. The system did not matter anymore. So, what was my system? I worked in a convenience store, which is the perfect job for a scratch-off gambler because after work, I'd start gambling. While working, I would watch to see what others bought and how long it has been since a winner or how many winners have been returned. I believed that I could get the winner during the time I was playing after work most of the time by what I thought was "playing the House." Unlike others, I was able to see what was bought, what was won, and what was lost throughout the day. At the end of the day, I had seen where the winners were likely to be. Sadly it seldom, if ever, worked, but I still believed in my "system." I believed it so much that I was gambling more and more as time went on. I became so tied into it that I believed that I was ahead and winning.

The lie that "I am a winner" became my personal hidden belief. I look back and realize that I was losing and losing a lot. The problem back when I was at the peak of my gambling is that I blocked out the loosing and only looked at what I won. My reality was not about the money by the end, and I point to the fact that when someone asked me about it, I could never say how much I had won or lost. So by the end, I would talk about my winning while scratching off tickets at the store in a small area where customers sat. Looking back, I can't believe that I believed the lie and shared that lie with others at the store.

Because I had some level of realization that I was losing it became clear that I had to set up a subconscious lie to myself to allow me to feel better about the losses. So because I was a winner I convinced myself that I would get ahead again. Thus my rationalizing the losses became "I'll win it all back." Winning back my losses became the rational for spending more and continually finding the money to use to win it back. For me, it was always in my mind to remember that "The next one would be the winner." These lies were important to keep me living in the fantasy. They set up the belief that helped avoid the reality that I was a compulsive gambler.

I became focused on winning it back and vested on getting the resources to do that at any cost. It led to the desire to keep going and believe falsely that I did not need to stop. Why would I stop? I believed I was on the verge of winning it all back, and even more importantly, I was going to win a lot more. As I grew weary of the chase for money I grew to enjoy the chase for the sake of the chase. At that point I began to believe that it was ok to gamble a little so then it promoted a new lie for me.

I believed that I could gamble "just a little bit." It is easy to keep going when I convinced myself that I was gambling just a little. Hey

I believed that gambling every day after work for one or two hours was just a little bit, so it was ok. Sadly, that is how I was gambling most of the time anyway, so I really did not have a problem... Right? Wrong! I needed to justify my escape somehow, and I enjoyed this form of escaping the best. I felt it was harmless and actually helpful in problem resolution for me.

That means that I was not gambling, I was just winding down after work. I was able to get away from my problems and "work" on a resolution to them in my own eyes. My view that I was just winding down after work and not really gambling was an illusion that made my gambling more dangerous because it opens me to lies to myself. It moved me to the next part of my world.

I am not like all those other gamblers…"I am not like the losers." What a mess that lie was because I go**t slapped** into reality after my first GA meeting on this lie. Earlier, I mentioned how I went to my first meeting, heard all these real stories of losses, left the meeting telling myself the lie, and when I bought a scratch-off ticket five minutes later, I came to reality. For about two years, I watched others come to the store I worked at and spend money on the lottery and told myself I was not like them. I watched them buy "numbers" and scratch-offs all the time, thinking that they were losing so much money, and my system was superior to what they were doing. The lie behind it was that I believed I was not like them. My realization was that I was exactly like those other gamblers and, in some cases, worse. Not all of the people I watched gamble were regular gamblers. This leads into the lie that I can pay back what I owe.

Remember that compulsive gambling is not all financial in nature, so not everything I owed was the financial. During my time of compulsive gambling, I was absent from my sons' lives at times. How does a person pay back not being there at times? Whatever I do, I will never be able to give back the time missed because it has passed. Compulsive gamblers have no way to go back and play with one of their children when they were five. Once the child is six I cannot go back in time and spend time with them when they were five. Compulsive gamblers lose these special moments. If they look at relationships with family, friends, and significant others, how does anyone get time back to spend it with these other people when you were gambling? The bottom line of believing they can pay back what they owe is that it focuses on the money and denies the other costs that cannot be recovered because they are not borrowing the time that never can be recovered.

The final lie to look at for the compulsive gambler is that those close to them will understand their absence while they are gone. The compulsive gambler, however, does not tell family and friends that they are gambling but rather make it sound like they are out working or some other activity. Often this is the hardest to cover up. It is hard to keep the lies straight and as a result, explaining inconsistencies, which show up at times and at the end when it all comes unraveled. The problem is that often there is someone in the compulsive gamblers life that is an enabler, and they often have their own lies to protect.

If the enabler is supportive of the gambler, their lies might start with "They are hard workers, and they need an outlet." That plays into the belief that they don't have that bad of a problem, so it's not a problem, which plays into the idea that when they go together, it is fun. These lies are a slippery slope for an enabling person.

This person may begin to enjoy the 'comps.' For those who don't know what 'comps' are, they are specials for 'high rollers.' If you are spending enough at the Casinos, they will send you 'free' nights, meals, house money, and other items to bring you back. Because the Casino has made a lot off the high roller, they make these available to them. In reality, compulsive gamblers have paid for these comps or are losing enough that they will. These 'comps' lead to an enabler beginning to overlook the flaws in the lies and grab onto one that is even grander. They build the self-justifying lie that there is nothing wrong with having a little fun (focused on gambling as the fun).

These lies are all foundational to the secrets held by the compulsive gambler and to those who are a part of their lives. The problem is that these secrets are not ones that are general in nature. They are individualized to the gambler's life and to the lives of those around them. Some of them may be shared, and some of them are personal. At this point, I can only address my own as they are ones I own as part of my recovery.

I will list a few of them but not all of them because of all the territory yet to cover and the secrets are better covered by the individual over time. Here are five of my secrets, or at least, I believed them to be secret.

1. I never believed that I was able to become addicted because when I started smoking. It was not a positive experience. I have gone back to it now and then, but because it affected my breathing negatively, I quit quickly.
2. I never considered compulsive behavior an addiction until my experience in recovery from gambling.
3. Because I watched my mother-in-law gamble, and I had seen others do it, I could not recognize it as an addiction.
4. I really believed I could avoid my problems by not addressing them with the person I felt drove me there.
5. I desired to be better than I was and struggled to meet what I believed would make my ex-wife happier.

These are hard to explain because they focus on self-image and what were personal perceptions for me. So I will move on, leaving you to think about the topic of secrets as you may find secrets that are not really secrets to those close to the addict. I do not want to plant ideas any further on the secrets aspect because for you it will help keep them personal.

Thoughts and Reflections

Thoughts and Reflections

Recovery

This is the road less traveled because an addict has a hard time finding it on their own, yet it cannot be forced upon them. It took me being suicidal to find the road to recovery. At that point, life is almost completely destroyed. Addicts have had court orders for treatment when it comes to substances but seldom if ever is it recommended for compulsive gamblers. Most compulsive gamblers lose the freedom noted by prison sentences when they are caught in schemes to get the needed money once the legitimate sources dry up. Others have committed suicide, and unless a person left clear connections to the gambling, it may not be linked. This can be seen by news reports of people who die at a casino or other place where they leave apology letters. Those who find the road to recovery have had a personal discovery or been at a point where they are found out by others and are guided to the path.

I found recovery through the threat of job loss followed by a family revelation and then a stay in an adult psych. unit. Once I left, I could have returned to my addiction, but thanks to GA and the fellowship there, I became aware of my addiction in a way that was irrefutable for me. Earlier, I told the story of my last bet after my first meeting, which is the final proof for me. Here is the longer version of it.

In late 2007, I was buying scratch-off tickets to avoid going home to my ex-wife because finances were a problem and led to arguments. Since I often worked shifts that were opposite of my ex, it was easy to make an excuse to avoid being there when she was awake or home. At some point, I was given three days pending, and while I was able to get my job back, there were consequences. I realized that I needed to explain something to my ex-wife. I did some of that but still kept secrets that put me on path to suicidal depression. The results were that I ended up being admitted to the psych unit for the depression and my ex-wife was able to look at stuff I had on my car and at the house without my interference, which led her to discover more about my gambling problem.

This made my depression worse and brought me home to an

angry wife ultimately. Upon release from the hospital, I was told I needed to get help. That help was in many forms, but ultimately, the biggest help came from the table of a GA meeting.

This is where I heard stories of losses, and took the twenty question test and passed it. After passing it with flying colors, hearing stories of the destruction brought on by the addiction, and then went on to blow my cover story that I was not that bad. I did that by driving out of the parking lot and to my favorite place to get gas where I bought a one dollar scratch-off ticket. This was unconscionable for me because I lost the ability to deny I had a problem in my eyes.

I have to believe that recovery is a process that starts because of the addict's lack of support for their unrealistic fantasy. Every addict has a different bubble burst in order to go into recovery and recovery never ends, it continues for life.

In time, the addict needs to begin working on making amends. This is the move that begins with themselves because they can't forgive others without forgiving themselves.

Thoughts and Reflections

Thoughts and Reflections

AMENDS!

There is a process to the amends that for me had to begin in my own 'skin.' I reached the point of wanting to die in order to avoid facing my disastrous results both for me and for those I affected. My earlier 'Open Letter' was because I realized that the worst destruction that was caused by my gambling were those who I affected without having ever met or been aware of. Imagine how hard it would be if you were a compulsive gambler, and you became a role model for others who would take on the addiction. Unlike other addictions, which are seen as addictions, compulsive gambling is not seen as a problem by most because of how 'helpful' it is for local economies and government entities.

Compulsive gamblers find themselves in a position exactly as any other addict when they reach the point of recovery with the exception that when it all ends, there is a lack of understanding of how they got there. People see the staggering alcoholic and the glassy eyed drug addict, but the compulsive gambler is not noticed until disaster hits. Making amends is difficult because almost no amount of change is acceptable, and it is not easy to get past what happened. Courts and non-gamblers will often say you could have just stopped. People may ask questions like:

- How could you spend that much?
- Don't you love your family?
- What is wrong with you?
- How could you be so blind to how much you spent?
- How could you miss…? Your…was so disappointed.
- Don't you care that we have lost the house?

For compulsive gamblers, these are the questions that need answers for significant others but mostly for themselves. Until the end, I never realized just how bad things were. When I started recovery, I had to find a way to stop the cycle that, years before, I said I would never do. I remembered the promise to myself, and it was as if I had failed twice by doing one thing. I told myself I would never do what I was doing, and I did it to the extent that I had caused myself to destroy everything around me. Sometimes amends cannot be done because they will be hurt as much or more by the realization of what was done. Amends are less about the past and more about the present and the future.

Amends are necessary as much for the addict as for those who were caught in the destructive wake. Many of the amends I did were not accepted as enough, or for the person, they were not the amends they wanted. These amends are for any person who was affected by the compulsive gambler's actions. Some, however, as I mentioned above are people you never met.

Even though amends are actively done, they are not always accepted and often the process lasts a lifetime.

Thoughts and Reflections

Thoughts and Reflections

A Lifetime of Work

Compulsive gamblers have not gotten where they are overnight, and they are not going to recover overnight. No matter how long it took to get to the point of beginning the process of recovery, the addict will have a lifetime of work to stay in recovery. The biggest problem with recovery is that even staying away from the addiction does not mean they will stay clean. Staying away from our original addiction is only part of the process. An addict needs to be vigilant all of their life because of cross addiction. It is not uncommon to recover from one addiction and just when everything seems to be better to pick up a new one. If you or someone you know is recovering from compulsive gambling, beware of that which becomes too fun or that seems to be taking hold of you.

Because of my awareness, here is what I believe is my list of addictions I have had personal experience with over the years.

- Eating
- Smoking
- Pop Drinking
- Shopping
- Computer
- Gambling

This is by no means a complete list of the possible addictions in my past and not all of them are done for me. I still spend a lot of time on the internet, eating and shopping at times. The hardest part of recovery for me is recognizing that I will never be done recovering. It is also hard to maintain certain activities that I need to keep doing and assessing if I am doing too much or if it is reasonable. Each day is truly the first day of recovery for me because I know if I stop believing that the problem is there, I take the chance of relapse.

Recovery is a lifetime job for any addict. There are problems with the gambling addict in that there are a lot of different ways to gamble and not all of them are accepted by compulsive gamblers as such. This means that relapse is much more probable. Those who have relapsed have the ability to keep it secret even from their fellow addicts because it is harder to see the signs.

Thoughts and Reflections

Thoughts and Reflections

Relapse

Here we are at a place where two truths are going to be addressed: that it is almost impossible to recover on your own and that without any support, it is inevitable that you will relapse.

On my own, I headed into my addiction without hesitation to my own destruction. Without any core support outside of myself it would be senseless to stop because it brought me a 'buzz.' If you are enjoying a piece of chocolate, and you have a whole candy bar are you going to stop at one bite? Most people would not stop at that one bite. Why? Because unless you have others who are there either to share it with or to set the limit of one bite, it makes no sense to you. There are people who can stop at one beer but on average since one beer does nothing for people they would not stop. It makes no sense to stop at one or two when it takes more than that to get the 'buzz' or feel you have achieved the effect you want.

The value of having others to be accountable to is that they will help you look at your addiction differently. I again refer back to my attendance at my first GA meeting. I heard the stories, but until I accepted my problem, it was not real to me.

When in recovery, a support system is absolutely necessary because an addict does not get to the bottom without a support system. Compulsive gamblers have other gamblers and or suppliers of the environment. In recovery, I realized how much I created a system that supported my compulsive gambling, so in order to have success in recovery, I need to surround myself with a support system as well.

The gambler's support system is a false one, so in recovery, they need a real one. That real one has to be composed of people who want them to get better. This is sometimes difficult because many of the people in their circle are from three central groups. The first are the promoters of the various forms of gambling. Next are other compulsive gamblers and lastly are people caught in the wake of the gamblers destruction. As a result, compulsive gamblers have a lot of problems building that support system. Some of this support system is completely out and others depend on the forgiveness factor.

Family members can be a great support. However, many compulsive gamblers have done the greatest harm to those people closest to them. Some hold out hope for their loved ones and become a part of the support system in recovery and others loose hope and need space. The compulsive gambler has a lot of work to do in recovery that is totally theirs to do. Part of that is figuring out the support system that is going to work best for them.

This all comes down to the desire of the compulsive gambler to surround themselves with people who are invested in recovery or to surround themselves with people who have different goals in mind. Clearly if you surround yourself with those who are stuck in the gambling world then that is the path you will follow. So the compulsive gambler fights for recovery, with the desire to return to their addiction ever present, as they look for their higher power in the will of their support system.

Without a support system, relapse is inevitable. Without the support of others, relapse is as likely to me as a compulsive eater in recovery at an all you can eat buffet. There is a problem that can crop up if you are not careful during recovery it is called cross addiction.

Thoughts and Reflections

Thoughts and Reflections

Cross Addiction

Cross addiction is what happens when an addict is in recovery and becomes addicted to something new. It is not always accepted by an addict that when they quit one addiction, they can end up with another, but realistically, if an addict does not accept the possibility of cross addiction, it is almost as inevitable as relapse. During the time compulsive gamblers are gambling, they may also be drinking alcohol, smoking, or over eating. So what happens is that as they recover from the compulsive gambling these other co-existing addictions tend to fill in the gaps. Often, it is either not noticed or some of the same false beliefs that supported a previous addiction begin to strengthen the new addiction.

As I stated earlier, there is a genetic predisposition for addiction, but it is my belief that it is generic in nature (a predisposition to addiction without a specific addiction). That is why I encourage compulsive gamblers to be aware of the potential for some new addiction to take them back down the path that they have traveled before. It is necessary for me to point out that the path may seem different, but the end result is the same as sure as the Earth revolves around the Sun. It is up to you where you go in your recovery and when you plan the route, be willing to accept route changes as needed to avoid going the same places even though the road is a new one.

Thoughts and Reflections

Co-Addictive Relationships

A co-addictive relationships can range from the couple who gambles together to two people who feed off the problems as a way to feel better about themselves. There are many types of co-addictive relationships, and each person has to look into this on his or her own to find them. I will attempt to list some of them from my perspective and experience but want to point out that this is from my own view.

Here is a list to start with:

- Co-Dependent Co-Addiction
- Dual Co-Addicted.
- Blind Addicted Enablers
- Enabling Addiction
- Double Blind Addiction
- Denial Addiction
- Openly Aware Addiction Supportive

Co-dependent co-addiction is a relationship where one person is focused on a relationship of total dependency to each other and the other is dependent on the addiction to cope with being co-dependent. In other words each person is dependent on the other and they are addicted to this codependent relationship as much to their chosen addiction.

Dual co-addicted - Two people who both enjoy the same addiction and do it together. It would seem this is the hardest situation to get into recovery because often the relationship has some basis in the addiction as the attraction.

Blind = Enablers - A person who enables the addict by not seeing it. They tend to not want to see it for fear of what they might find out. The addict is eager to please that denial because they don't see what they are doing as a problem.

Enabling Addiction - The enabler in this relationship is fully aware of the addiction and may even be a supplier to help promote the addiction.

Double Blind Addiction – This is the case of two people who are both in the addiction and neither of them sees it as a problem.

Denial Addiction – One person is aware of the addiction but \ denies it exists. The other simply enjoys the addiction but does not believe it is an addiction.

Openly Aware Addiction Supportive - Both people in this relationship are aware of the addiction and could care less to avoid it. The addiction is a part of the relationship like going to dinner. No one is ready to change, and for this relationship, the only way anything is going to change is if there is a major disaster related to the problem.

Thoughts and Reflections

Thoughts and Reflections

Final Points and a Summary of My Recovery Today

At this point I want to talk about how compulsive gamblers might attempt to hide the financial and other problems as they became more obvious to those around them. Below is a list of possible things that might be done. These are not meant to be hurtful and may be done by others who are not gamblers with a problem.

1. Intercepting the mail.
2. Shredding bills and collection notices.
3. Failing to answer their cell phones while in the throes of their gambling.
4. Talking about their big wins but being silent when they lost.
5. Taking extra cash with them, so they can claim to have won it if asked.
6. Shuffle money in accounts.
7. If they have access to funds, there is the possibility of 'borrowing" money with the intention of paying it back before it is noticed, which may lead to being charged with criminal actions such as embezzlement, theft, and/or perjury.
8. If it gets bad enough, they might attempt suicide to get out of the problems.
9. Different types of crimes of desperation, which under normal situations would never be considered by the person.
10. Lying about where they are and missing work as a result.

The best way to learn about the person is to help them get help. This list is small and leaves room for other things. Sadly not everyone gets to experience their bottom the same way. Unlike other addictions, the symptoms are not always going to be visible to those around them.

My bottom was explained earlier in this book. Sadly the losses that were the hardest for me were ones people don't often realize are there. I am blessed that I have two sons and a number of family members that I believed I had lost that are still a part of my life.

So now I leave it up to you to decide if you believe in the addiction of Compulsive Gambling. This leaves you two choices.

1. Deny the existence of the addiction and do nothing.
2. Believe the existence of compulsive gambling and help others understand that it exists.

Thoughts and Reflections

Thoughts and Reflections